First Steps

an excerpt from

Follow

Learning to Follow Jesus

by
Daniel McNaughton
and
Bryan Koch

WWW.LEARNINGTOFOLLOW.NET

Morning Joy Media
Spring City, Pennsylvania

Copyright © 2010, 2011 by Daniel McNaughton, Bryan Koch

Excerpted by permission from *Follow: Learning to Follow Jesus* by Daniel McNaughton and Bryan Koch.

All rights reserved. No portion of this book may be reproduced, stored in a retrieval system, or transmitted in any form or by any means—electronic, mechanical, photocopy, recording, scanning, or other—except for brief quotations in reviews or articles, without the prior written permission of the author.

Published by Morning Joy Media.

Visit www.morningjoymedia.com for more information on bulk discounts and special promotions, or e-mail your questions to info@morningjoymedia.com.

Unless otherwise noted, Scripture quotations are taken from the Holy Bible, New International Version®, NIV®. Copyright © 1973, 1978, 1984 by Biblica, Inc.™ Used by permission of Zondervan. All rights reserved worldwide.

Cover Design: Staci Focht
Interior Design: Debbie Capeci
Author Photos: Dan Desrosiers and Dave Zerbe Studio

Cataloging-In-Publication Data

Subject Headings:
1. Discipling (Christianity) 2. Spiritual formation. 3. Christian life.

ISBN 978-1-937107-02-4

Printed in the United States of America

Contents

4	Getting Started
	An Overview of the Attributes
8	Attribute One: Learn to Be With Jesus
11	Attribute Two: Learn to Listen
14	Attribute Three: Learn to Heal
18	Attribute Four: Learn to Influence
21	Attribute Five: Learn to Love
24	Attribute Six: Learn to Pray
28	Attribute Seven: Learn to Manage
31	Attributes Overview: Decisions
32	Notes

GETTING STARTED

CONGRATULATIONS ON YOUR DECISION to become a follower of Jesus! You may or may not realize it yet, but following Jesus is the most important decision you will ever make in your life. It will affect every future decision you will make on this earth, and it will affect where you spend eternity. You have made a great decision! This book is designed to help you develop in your walk with Christ so you can know and honor God the rest of your life and for eternity.

Since it is such an important decision, it is worthwhile to take a few minutes to review what it means to become a follower of Jesus. John 1:12 describes becoming part of God's family as a two-part decision: "Yet to all who received him [Jesus], to those who believed in his name, he gave the right to become children of God." You must **receive** Christ and **believe** in his name. Even though the Bible teaches that Jesus created the universe (John 1:3), he never forces anyone to follow him. God gives you freedom to accept or reject Jesus. By receiving Jesus, you accept that he was God, that he was the perfect representation of what God is like. By believing in his name, you are trusting that Jesus paid the price for your sin when he died on the cross. John 3:16 says, "For God so loved the world that he gave his one and only Son, that whoever believes in him shall not perish but have eternal life." God came to earth because he loves every one of us and wants us to have eternal life. Jesus describes eternal life this way in John 17:3, "Now this is eternal life: that they may know you, the only true God, and Jesus Christ, whom you have sent." Eternal life is knowing Jesus. If you are uncertain whether or not you have done that, why not take a

Getting Started

minute right now and make sure. If you are unaccustomed to praying or if you are unsure what to pray, you can join me in the following prayer.

Prayer:
Dear Heavenly Father, I want to become a follower of Jesus. I receive Jesus into my life. I believe he was God and that he came to pay the price for my sin when he died on the cross. Please forgive me for living life my own way. I turn away from that life and I turn toward you. As best I know how and with your help, I want to live for you from this day forward. Amen.

Having received Jesus and believed what he came to do, you can now be certain that you are part of God's family.

There are a few things that are important to keep in mind from the beginning. First, becoming a follower of Jesus is not just about learning information. It is much more than that. Jesus said that those who come to him, hear his words, and put them into practice will be the ones who will have a foundation on which to stand when tough times come. Building a solid foundation requires you to bring everything to Christ, hear God's Word, and then put it into practice.

Second, most of us learn best from watching and learning from others. In other words, "more is caught than is taught." That's why we encourage you to put yourself in four contexts where you can learn from others: a large gathering where you can worship God and hear Bible teaching (a church service); a small group where you can apply the Bible to your life and live out your faith with others; a one-on-one mentoring meeting with a spiritual coach; and a private time with God on your own. *First Steps*[1] is a tool that can help you develop in your private time with God and can serve as a discussion starter with you and your coach. We all need

Learning to Follow Jesus

people with whom we can share our honest thoughts, our successes, our failures, and our questions, especially when we are just starting out on a new venture. A spiritual coach and the people in your small group will help you learn how to honor God in every area of life. They will probably not have all the answers to your questions, but they may serve as resources to you, and they are committed to sharing what they know with you.

What church do you plan to attend?............................

Would you like a spiritual coach?...............................

Would you like more information about small groups?....

If you don't have a spiritual coach or a small group yet, please contact a pastor to help you find both.

Third, following Christ is a process. You will not be perfect, nor will your spiritual coach or the members of your small group. Only Jesus is perfect. When you follow Christ, you accept what he has done for you. Knowing that your eternal destiny depends on Jesus' righteousness and not yours will set you free from trying to work to get God to love you. Jesus has already pleased God for you. There is nothing you can ever do to make God love you more. His love for you is limitless and eternal. His thoughts about you are always good. Enjoy your newfound reality of knowing God is pleased with you because of Jesus. Don't try to work to please him. Just live your life in gratitude for his amazing love and acceptance. As you spend time with other followers of Christ and with your loving Heavenly Father, you will discover that you want to become more like Christ, and you will change. God will change you.

This book is designed to help you cultivate good habits that will support a healthy spiritual environment for your new walk with Christ. To get the most out of this tool, you will need to make the following choices:

Getting Started

- Set aside about fifteen minutes per day to focus on your spiritual growth. Every relationship takes time. Your relationship with Christ is no exception. Choose a time slot that will work consistently for you. Many people find that the morning is best. Others believe the time before they go to bed is best. Some people do both. The most important thing is that you make time for your spiritual growth. You may have to experiment but pick a time that works for you. What time will work best for you on a daily basis?
  ....

- Write your answers in the book. You will retain more of what you are learning if you take the time to write your answers.

- Read the Bible references for yourself. If you don't have a Bible in a modern translation (New International Version [NIV] and New Living Translation [NLT] are good ones), ask your spiritual coach to help you find one. What translation will you use?
  ....

- Memorize the verses linked with each attribute. Do your best to learn them word-for-word. If you take a little time each day, you will discover they will come to mind much easier. Review all previously memorized verses daily; that puts them into your long-term memory. You won't regret it.

- Put what you learn into practice right away. A follower of Jesus is one who learns what Jesus is like and then takes action to become like him. Enjoy the journey.

ATTRIBUTE ONE · OVERVIEW
Learn to Be With Jesus

Scripture Memory (new):

"Come, follow me," Jesus said, "and I will make you fishers of men." Matthew 4:19

Read: Matthew 4:18–22

ONE OF THE FIRST THINGS we learn when we become followers of Jesus is he wants us to be with him.

What did Jesus say to Peter and Andrew in Matthew 4:18–22? ....

Notice that Jesus took the initiative in their relationship. He loved them and he loves you as well. He is and has been reaching out to you from the time you were born. He invites you to follow him—to be with him.

In John's Gospel in chapter 1, we also see Jesus inviting people to be with him. Andrew started following Jesus after John the Baptist said Jesus was "the Lamb of God who takes away the sin of the world." When Jesus saw Andrew following him, he asked, "What do you want?" Andrew responded by calling Jesus "Teacher" and asking where he was staying. Jesus invited him, "Come and see" and they spent the whole day together. There is no higher calling in life than Jesus' call to be with him. You may do great things for him. You may help many people learn to follow him and that's great, but your primary calling is just to be with him.

Attribute 1 • Learn to Be With Jesus

Does it surprise you that the Creator of the universe invites us to be with him? The psalmist writes, "What is man that you are mindful of him, the son of man that you care for him?" (Psalm 8:4). God cares about you and wants you to be close to him. How does it make you feel to know that Jesus wants you to be with him? (Pause right now and take a few minutes to thank the Lord for calling you to follow him. Tell him how you feel and affirm your commitment to follow him.)

What are some of your feelings about Jesus' calling you to be one of his followers? ....
....
....

What did Peter, Andrew, James and John have to leave behind to follow Jesus? ....
....
....

What would be tough for you to leave behind to follow him? ....
....

While it may seem tough to leave something behind right now, you will soon realize that nothing you leave behind can compare in value to the amazing gift that you have as a follower of Jesus.

In Matthew 13:44–46 Jesus compares finding the kingdom of God (having Christ rule in your heart) to a man who found a treasure in a field. He hid the treasure and then in his great joy went and sold all he had and bought that field. He also compared it to a merchant who found a pearl of great value and went away and sold everything he had and bought it. Nothing you have can compare with the treasure you have when you follow Jesus.

One of the best parts about following Jesus is that he will never leave you. The last words in the book of Matthew say

Learning to Follow Jesus

this, "And surely I am with you always, to the very end of the age." Jesus' commitment to be with you is a forever thing. Though others leave you or don't fulfill their commitments to you, Jesus promises that he will always be with you both now and throughout eternity. You will never be alone again.

What did Jesus say would happen if Peter and Andrew followed him?..
....

Following Jesus will change your life. He promised to transform his disciples from being fishermen who could catch fish to fishermen who would catch people. He will transform your life as well so you can become the person he designed you to be. You may not know what that is just yet, but it will become clear as you follow him. There is one thing you can be sure of, however: Jesus will lead you to make a difference in the lives of others. That was his purpose for coming, and it was the one thing he told his disciples to do as he was leaving. Don't let that intimidate you. It will be a wonderful and fulfilling journey. He will show you the next steps, and he will always be with you. Just enjoy being with him now.

Prayer:
Heavenly Father, thank you for inviting me to follow you. It amazes me that you care about me enough to want to be with me. I respond to your invitation again and declare that I am your follower. I will joyfully leave behind the things you ask me to because I believe that I will be better off with you. Change me into the person you want me to become. I rest in your commitment to be with me forever. I also rest in your presence right now, my heart's true home. Amen.

ATTRIBUTE TWO · OVERVIEW
Learn to Listen

Scripture Memory:

"Come, _____ me," Jesus _____, "and I will make you _____ of men." Matthew ___:19

"Come, follow me," Jesus said, "and I will make you fishers of men." Matthew 4:19

Read: Matthew 4:23–25

JESUS BEGAN TEACHING his followers by inviting them to observe what he was doing. According to these verses, what did the first followers of Jesus observe him doing? _____

As a follower of Jesus, it is important for you to observe Jesus' teaching, preaching, and healing as well. (We'll talk about Jesus' healing in the next attribute.) You will find a summary of Jesus' preaching in Matthew 4:17: "From that time on Jesus began to preach, 'Repent, for the kingdom of heaven is near.'" There are a couple of terms that need defining. First, the word "repent" means "to turn away from something and to turn toward something else." When some people hear the word "repent" they think of it negatively. Perhaps it stirs up an image of a screaming evangelist. Repentance, however, is positive. When we repent we get to turn away from the things that are keeping us from following

Christ, and then turn to him, the Author of life.

Second, "the kingdom of heaven" means that God can have first place in your heart. I don't know what comes to your mind when you think of "kingdom," but I think of walled cities, castles and kings, like the Battle of Helms Deep in the movie *Lord of the Rings: The Two Towers*. The kingdom of heaven is different from that. God's kingdom is not about weapons and war machines, but there is a king. Luke 17:20b–21 states, "The kingdom of God does not come with your careful observation, nor will people say, 'Here it is,' or 'There it is,' because the kingdom of God is within you." When the kingdom of God comes in your life, he rules your heart. Your life will change, not by force but by the power of God. We can change because Jesus is near to help us and empower us. That's great news.

Matthew 4:23 describes Jesus' preaching about the kingdom like that. The fact that we can turn away from our old lives and have God rule in our hearts is great news. But it's not without a cost. Your priorities will change as you make room for God to rule in your life. You know what rules your heart by where you give your treasures: your time, your talent, and your money.

What would you say are the top priorities in your life right now? ....
....

What are some things you need to turn away from (repent) so that Christ can rule in your heart? ....
....

Repentance is ongoing for a follower of Christ. No one will ever be perfect except Jesus. As you get to know Jesus better, repentance will become easier because you will realize that his ways are always best!

What good things could happen if you were to repent from these things? ....

Attribute 2 • Learn to Listen

What are some things from which you would like to repent?

I want to repent from: I can turn from this and to God by:
1................................   ....
2................................   ....
3................................   ....

You may want to share these with your spiritual coach, who can encourage you in your decisions. Your spiritual coach is going through the same process, so you don't need to worry about what he or she will think of you. Romans 3:23 reminds us that "All have sinned and fall short of the glory of God." There's another great passage about this as well in 1 John 1:8–10:

> If we claim to be without sin, we deceive ourselves and the truth is not in us. If we confess our sins, he is faithful and just and will forgive us our sins and purify us from all unrighteousness. If we claim we have not sinned, we make him out to be a liar and his word has no place in our lives.

Repentance just brings these things to light so we can deal with them, with God's help. Remember, he is with you.

Prayer:

Dear Jesus, thank you for the invitation to turn away from my old life. I do actively turn away from the things I have done that are wrong and I turn to you. I repent from [tell God the things you mentioned previously]. Thank you for replacing those things with your leadership in my life. I welcome you into my life. Thank you also for inviting me to bring my pain to you. Please bring healing to my life in every way. I am so grateful to you for helping me find life in you, Jesus Christ. Amen.

ATTRIBUTE THREE · OVERVIEW
Learn to Heal

Scripture Memory:
"_____, follow ____ ," Jesus said, "_____ I will _____ you fishers of _____." Matthew ___ : ___

"Come, follow me," Jesus said, "and I will make you fishers of men." Matthew 4:19

Read: Matthew 4:23–25

As I was looking at Jesus' method for helping people learn to follow him, it struck me that one of the first things he did was invite his followers to be with him while he preached and healed people. There is nothing like seeing God heal firsthand. Based on these verses, what kinds of things did Jesus heal?[1]

During the summer of 1982, I (Bryan) was blessed to live my lifelong dream of being a professional baseball player when I was drafted by the Chicago White Sox and joined their farm system. Those years would become some of the most exciting times of my life. As I walked onto a professional baseball field for the first time, I could not help but remember playing sandlot games with my neighborhood friends and pretending to be Johnny Bench or some other major league great. After three years of enjoying the culture of minor league baseball, the cheers of the crowd ended when

Attribute 3 • Learn to Heal

a fastball hit me in the left eye. As I fell across home plate attempting to regain my senses, little did I know that this injury would end my career and dreams of being a big league player. After several visits and consultations with doctors from around the country, I learned that I had not only lost my career, but also about seventy-five percent of my vision in that eye.

A lifetime of vision problems became worse in the summer of 2006 when I awoke with irritation and pain in my right eye—the good one. Thinking it was a minor problem, I scheduled an appointment with my eye doctor only to find out that the irritation was caused by my contact lens tearing a hole in the very center of my cornea. My emotions went from "no big deal" to the fear of "I could lose my sight." My doctor was concerned that even if the hole in my cornea healed, the remaining scar tissue could still impair my vision. Coupled with the injury to my left eye, the prognosis was grim. My family and my congregation began to pray and intercede for my healing and that is exactly what happened. Jesus Christ healed and restored my right eye. Not only did Jesus heal the hole in my cornea, but he also removed all traces of scar tissue, to my doctor's amazement.

When I (Daniel) was about five years old, I also experienced a dramatic healing. I was trying to get some glue in a high cabinet in our home by using the drawers below as steps. When my foot slipped, I hung my arm inside one of the drawers and broke a bone around my elbow. As we were scurrying around to go to the hospital, Nina Gaddis, a guest speaker who was staying at our home, prayed for my arm and God healed it. I'll never forget her quietly asking God to heal my arm while she lightly touched it. As she prayed, my arm immediately stopped hurting and returned to a normal appearance. That experience shaped how I think about God's miraculous intervention.

Learning to Follow Jesus

Fast-forward to the second year of my doctoral program (1987–1988) at the University of Toronto. I took a class entitled, "Synoptic Miracles." The professor began that course by making a statement similar to the following:

> No one in the twentieth century with a thinking mind could possibly believe in a virgin birth, miracles, or the bodily resurrection. We know these things don't happen. So when we read the miracle stories of the Bible, we are not talking about what happened. We are reading perhaps what they thought happened but not what actually happened.

Based on that assumption, he proceeded to explain how we need to demythologize the stories of Jesus to get to the real, historical Jesus. I remember walking through this thought process: "I'm definitely in the twentieth century. I believe I have a thinking mind. I am engaged fully in the academic process and excelling. And, I not only believe in miracles, I have experienced them." I understand skepticism. I have my own struggles with it, but I had never encountered someone who said it just couldn't have happened. Needless to say, that was a fascinating semester for the both of us. I challenged his worldview and he challenged mine. I'll share more of my journey about that in the following pages.

As you begin to follow Jesus, be open to God's supernatural intervention in your life. Talk with God throughout your day with words of love, praise, and need. It's not about the formality of your prayer, but the sincerity of your heart. Just ask God to do the miraculous, place your faith in him, and see what happens.

While you are pondering that thought, consider that there are eighty-eight references in the New Testament to healing. Some of them are stories of Jesus healing someone. Others, however, refer to God healing people through the prayers of his followers (Luke 9:2, 9:6; Acts 3:16, 4:9–30, 5:16, 8:7, 9:34, 10:38, 14:9, 28:8). In fact, 1 Corinthians 12:9 refers to "gifts of healing" being given to some of Christ's

Attribute 3 • Learn to Heal

followers. You need to know that since Christ lives in you, he can provide healing through you. Begin to pray and ask him to meet needs about which you are aware.

We all need healing. You may need physical or emotional healing. You might need healing in a relationship. We all need spiritual healing. Whatever your need, you can bring it to the Lord and ask him. I wish I understood why God chooses to heal sometimes and not others, but I do not. But you never want it to be said about you that you could have had healing but you didn't ask. So ask and trust God.

What kinds of things do you need healing for today?

....
....
....

Share these with your spiritual coach, who will agree with you in prayer for your healing.

Prayer:
Thank you, Heavenly Father, for reminding me that you care about the details of my life. I praise you and thank you for the new life you are giving me through Jesus. In response to what I am reading today, I ask you for healing for [name the areas for which you want healing]. (Describe how the problem has caused you pain or suffering. Tell it to God even though he already knows.) Your Word tells me that you are compassionate toward me and that you care about me. I ask that you would have mercy on me about [name the area]. I trust that you love me and care about me. Thank you for your kindness to me. In Jesus' name I pray, amen.

Attribute Four · Overview
Learn to Influence

Scripture Memory:

"Come, _____ _____ ," Jesus said, " _____ _____ _____ you _____ of men." _____ _____ : _____

"*Come, follow me,*" *Jesus said, "and I will make you fishers of men.*" Matthew 4:19

Read: Matthew 5:13–16

WHO ARE YOU? And why are you here? Many people spend their whole lives not ever knowing why they are on the planet. At the beginning of his teaching Jesus clearly defines who we are as his followers.

What two metaphors does Jesus use to describe his followers? _____

Both of these metaphors describe our identity as influencers for God. Salt preserves things and makes our food taste better. When it comes in contact with something it has an effect. Light helps us see things more clearly, especially when it is dark. The reason we are on this planet is to impact people for God. We are not here for ourselves. As Rick Warren so aptly puts it:

> It's not about you. The purpose of your life is far greater than your own personal fulfillment, your peace of mind, or even your happiness. It's far greater than your family, your career, or

Attribute 4 • Learn to Influence

even your wildest dreams and ambitions. If you want to know why you were placed on this planet, you must start with God. You were born *by* his purpose and *for* his purpose.[1]

The ultimate goal for everything you do is to influence people for God so they might also praise God in heaven. You are an attractor for God.

This thought could be a bit overwhelming. You might say, "How can I ever attract people to God? My life is not perfect enough to point people to God." The answer? God will attract people to himself through your life as you continue to learn to follow him. Of course you are not perfect, but he is. As God begins to change you, people will notice and they may want to know how that happened.

Have you ever noticed that when you hang out with someone you become like them? Do you have a friend with whom you share special vocabulary or a favorite handshake or similar jokes? The same will become true with you and Jesus. As you are with him, you will start to become more and more like him. For most of us, this is such a gradual process that we may not even see it, but others will. And when they do, we are living up to our identity as salt and light.

Make a list of friends, family, neighbors, and co-workers who could benefit from becoming followers of Jesus.

Learning to Follow Jesus

Prayer:
Heavenly Father, thank you for defining who I am and why I'm on this planet. Life is starting to make sense. I really want you to influence people through my life. Continue to change me so that I reflect you clearly. I know I can't do this on my own and you are not asking me to. I rest in our relationship right now. You are so good. I bring my friends and family to you now. Would you pull them to you? Would you open their eyes to see how empty their lives are without you? Would you help them see their need for a forever relationship with you? Remove any confusion or barriers that would keep them from getting to know you. Help my life to be attractive for you. Give me wisdom to know how to approach these relationships. Help me to love them. I bring them to you. Amen.

ATTRIBUTE FIVE · OVERVIEW
Learn to Love

Scripture Memory:

"Come, ———— ——," ———— ————, "and I — ———— ———— ———— ———— ————." ———— ————: ————

"Come, follow me," Jesus said, "and I will make you fishers of men." Matthew 4:19

Read: Matthew 5:43–48

FOLLOWERS OF JESUS LEARN from the beginning and all throughout their lives that love is the foundation for everything. Many people think that loving God is only a personal and private thing. While loving God is both personal and private, it is not only that. Loving God will also lead you to love people. What two commands does Jesus make in Matthew 5:44? ....
....

If you wrote, "love your enemies" and "pray for those who persecute you," you are correct. According to Matthew 5:45, what does Jesus say will happen if we obey him in these commands? ....
....

One thing that identifies an authentic follower of Jesus is love for others. As you are learning to follow, it may seem quite foreign to you that you could love people who have

Learning to Follow Jesus

hurt you. If you have people who have caused you pain in your past whom you find difficult to love, I have good news for you. Jesus will enable you to rise above your past hurts. As you get to know Jesus better and as you learn to trust and obey him, you will find great freedom. *Follow* can help you take steps in that direction.[1] You will pour out your heart to God and you will enjoy the kindness and the compassion of God as he heals you.

Today's challenge, however, is actually a decision only you can make. Will you obey Jesus' commands in Matthew 5:43–48 to love your enemies and pray for those who persecute you? As you are thinking about this, I want you to know a couple of things. First, the type of love Jesus is talking about is not a feeling. Love means you do what is best for the other person regardless of how you or they feel about it. It is choosing to see that person as someone Jesus loves. As such, it is a decision. Choosing to love someone who had hurt me would never have happened in my life if Jesus did not teach me to do it. I would never have considered it. It is not logical or normal for me to do good to my enemies. Second, loving someone does not necessarily mean that you do what the other person wants. That would not always be loving. For example, it is not the most loving thing to allow abusive people to continue to abuse you. The most loving thing might be for you to help those people experience the consequences of their actions. Third, the only way you are going to be able to love people the way they need to be loved, especially your enemies, is with Jesus' help. That's why you pray for them. Tell God your honest feelings about those people and what you want to happen to them (good or bad).

As you open up this dialogue with God, a wonderful thing will happen. Your capacity to love God will grow as will your capacity to love people. You will also discover that your responses to people can be independent of their

Attribute 5 • Learn to Love

actions and their responses toward you. You may even find yourself starting to feel compassion toward them. You may not like them, but you will be able to love them. I have found great freedom in knowing I do not have to hate my enemies anymore.

Having encouraged you, it is time now to act. For whom do you need to pray? ....
....

Join with me now as we pray.

Prayer:

Heavenly Father, you are challenging me today to do something that goes against my nature, to love my enemies. I confess I have not done that in the past, but I want to learn from you how to do that. I pray now for [mention the person's name]. [Say his name] became my enemy when he [tell God what the person did to hurt you even though God already knows.] You know how that hurt me and the decisions I made because of that. I bring that to you right now. Continue the healing process in my life. I know that you love [mention the name] and that you want the best for his life. I ask that your plan for him will be accomplished. Help me to act in loving ways toward [name] in the future. Teach me how to love like you love. Amen.

ATTRIBUTE SIX · OVERVIEW
Learn to Pray

Scripture Memory:

" _____ , _____ , " _____ _____ , " _____
_____ _____ _____ _____ _____ _____ .
_____ _____ : _____

"Come, follow me," Jesus said, "and I will make you fishers of men." Matthew 4:19

Read: Matthew 6:5–15

JESUS' FOLLOWERS didn't follow him long before they realized that prayer was important and normal for him. Luke 5:16 says this, "But Jesus often withdrew to lonely places and prayed." As a follower of Jesus, it will become normal for you to pray as well. In this passage, Jesus is contrasting good prayer and bad prayer.

What is the difference between good and bad prayer?

....
....
....

In Matthew 6:9–13, Jesus teaches his followers how to pray. The Lord's Prayer is not intended to be a rote prayer that is prayed over and over but rather is an example of how to pray. Think about prayer more as a conversation between two friends, not a formula. You can talk with God about anything. Feel free to use your own words to express your thoughts and concerns to God. Notice the components of this simple prayer:

- **Relationship**—"Our Father in heaven" teaches us that we are in a loving relationship with our Heavenly Father and with others as well who are part of the family.
- **Respect**—"Hallowed be your name" teaches us that God is holy and as such must receive honor and respect. Tell the Lord how much he means to you and honor him.
- **Reign**—"Let your kingdom come" teaches us that we start with what God wants. He wants to rule in our hearts. When we pray "let your kingdom come," we are inviting him be our leader and our guide. We bow our lives before him when we pray, "let your kingdom come."
- **Food**—"Give us today our daily bread" teaches us that we can ask God to meet our basic needs today. When our lives are lined up with his values, we can ask for fuel to do it.
- **Forgiveness**—"Forgive us our debts as we also have forgiven our debtors" teaches us that when we pray we remember we need forgiveness as much as everyone else. God expects us to model to others the forgiveness he gives to us. In fact, this is so important for us that God requires us to forgive others in order for us to receive his forgiveness. This is important!
- **Freedom**—"And lead us not into temptation but deliver us from the evil one" teaches us that God can help us be victorious in every temptation. With God's help we can be delivered from the things that are destroying us.

Learning to Follow Jesus

Where does Jesus say his followers should go when we pray? ....
....

It's really important to find a quiet place and a time that you can be alone to pray. There are many ways to do this. You can get up a few minutes earlier than usual, perhaps before others get out of bed. Or, you can go for a walk in the neighborhood.

When and where do you plan to pray? ....
....

You will want to set aside time each day to follow Jesus in prayer. Start with a small amount of time, perhaps five to ten minutes. Eventually, you will probably increase the time but for now set aside at least five minutes. You learn to pray by praying. Feel free to use the six components of the Lord's Prayer to direct your thoughts and words to God. Use your own words to express your thoughts to God. Prayer is not a magic formula. It's just a friend talking with a friend.

As you talk with God, take a few minutes to listen to him as well. Rarely does God speak audibly. In fact, it has never happened to me. But I do have thoughts and impressions that come to me occasionally when I pray, and I have learned that's one of the ways he speaks to me. If you think God might be speaking to you, take a moment to write it down and test it out. One good test is whether it is consistent with what God says elsewhere in his Word. God never contradicts himself. You may not yet know whether what you hear is God or not so feel free to share it with your spiritual coach or a pastor to confirm it. You will learn to tell the difference between what God is speaking and what are just your thoughts.

Prayer:
God, it is great to know I am part of your family and that you are my loving heavenly Father. I give you honor.

Attribute 6 • Learn to Pray

Truly there is no one like you. I respect you more than I can adequately express with my own words. Please rule my life. Lead me today. Thank you for your provisions for my life. I have everything I really need. Forgive me where I have done wrong. (Go ahead and mention specific things for which you know you need forgiveness.) I choose to extend your forgiveness to everyone around me as well, Lord, because you have been so gracious to me. Lead me away from doing the things I know are destructive and to a path of freedom today. It's great having you in my life. Amen.

Attribute Seven · Overview
Learn to Manage

Scripture Memory:

" _____ , _____ , " _____ , "
_____ _____ _____ _____ _____ _____ ."
_____ _____ : _____

"Come, follow me," Jesus said, "and I will make you fishers of men." Matthew 4:19

Read: *Matthew 6:19–24*

WHAT WOULD YOU CONSIDER to be your treasure? For some of us, it is definitely our money. For others, it's reputation. Or time off. Or shoes. Really! I (Daniel) have a box of treasures; actually, several stashes of treasures. We have moved that box from place to place—a Punt, Pass and Kick trophy from the second grade, class certificates from the fifth grade, my first athletic letter when I was in seventh grade, some pictures and newspaper clippings of years as a basketball player. Treasures. Stuff! I got into the box not that long ago and realized several of the trophies were broken. The paper clippings are yellowing. They are simply not going to last.

Jesus is kind enough and direct enough to address the issue of what we treasure early in our lives as followers. He wants the best for us, and he can't bear for us to waste time and energy on things that simply aren't part of our trip as a follower.

Attribute 7 • Learn to Manage

What kinds of things does Jesus say we should not store up?

What are some examples of things that moths can eat, rust can destroy, and thieves can steal?

What reason does Jesus give for not storing up these things?

What kinds of things does Jesus say we should store up?

What reason does Jesus give for storing up these things?

You must not miss Jesus' statement, "For where your treasure is, there your heart will be also." He does *not* say as many think, "For where your heart is, there your treasure will be also." He says the opposite. In other words, where you put your treasure, that's where your heart will go. Your treasures really are your time, your talent, and your money. He's saying that where you choose to invest your treasure, you will discover your heart will follow. Your heart is submissive to your treasure. He says it blatantly in verse 24, "You cannot serve both God and money." It's impossible to love both. You have to make a choice.

This was a tough one for me early in my walk with Christ. We always had lots of food on the table and adequate clothing, but I grew up thinking that I needed and wanted to have a lot more. It became somewhat of an obsession. I wanted to be wealthy. Although my father was a minister, I didn't even consider being a minister because I was convinced I could not make the kind of money I wanted. I had to surrender my desire to make lots of money when I became a follower of Jesus. You will, too. It's one of the best decisions I have ever made. God supplies everything I need. I am certain I have

Learning to Follow Jesus

also enjoyed the resources he has given me far more than if I had not surrendered. I am confident you will too. And it all makes sense based on what we have already learned as a follower. We exist for him and we fulfill our purpose in this life when we use his resources to join what he is doing in the world. The psalmist says it this way in Psalm 24:1, "The earth is the LORD's, and everything in it." That's another way of saying, "It's all God's."

What kinds of things do you treasure that you need to surrender to God?

What are some places or areas of your life in which you need to invest so that your heart goes where you want it to go?

What are you going to invest in each of these areas?

Share your decisions with your spiritual coach this week. Ask your spiritual coach how she invests her treasures (time, talent, and money) so that her heart lines up with God's purposes in the world. Also, ask her what has happened as a result of these investments.

Prayer:
Jesus, thank you for telling me the truth about my treasures. I choose to serve you and not money. Help me to be courageous enough to invest in things that I know will matter to you. Help me to stop investing in things that won't matter one second after I pass from this life. I give this whole area of treasures over to you. I trust you with my life and my treasure. Amen.

Attribute Seven
Decisions

Notes

Getting Started
1. *First Steps* is an excerpt from *Follow: Learning to Follow Jesus* by Daniel McNaughton and Bryan Koch (Spring City, PA: Morning Joy Media, 2011).

Attribute Three • Overview
1. There was nothing that Jesus could not heal. Jesus healed diseases and sicknesses. He also set people free who were dominated by forces of evil.

Attribute Four • Overview
1. Rick Warren, *The Purpose-Driven Life* (Grand Rapids: Zondervan, 2002), 17.

Attribute Five • Overview
1. Daniel McNaughton and Bryan Koch, "Attribute Six–Learn to Pray, Step 4 –Learning to Pray Through Pain" in *Follow: Learning to Follow Jesus* (Spring City, PA: Morning Joy Media, 2011), 173–177.

If ***First Steps*** helped you grow in your walk with God, you will want to continue with Daniel and Bryan's book ***Follow: Learning to Follow Jesus***. ***Follow*** provides practical, step-by-step processes that will help you incorporate the attributes of ***First Steps*** into your walk with God. It also includes spiritual coaching guides and resources that show you how to share what you are learning with others.

If you are interested in ordering ***Follow: Learning to Follow Jesus***, please visit **www.learningtofollow.net**. You may also contact the publisher, Morning Joy Media, whose information is located on the copyright page of this excerpt.